DISEASE
UPDATE

The **Tuberculosis** Update

Alvin and Virginia Silverstein and Laura Silverstein Nunn

Enslow Publishers, Inc.
40 Industrial Road   PO Box 38
Box 398   Aldershot
Berkeley Heights, NJ 07922 Hants GU12 6BP
USA   UK
http://www.enslow.com

Acknowledgments

The authors thank Anne Marie Van Hoven, M.D., and Laura Willett, M.D., for their careful reading of the manuscript and their many helpful comments and suggestions.

Library of Congress Cataloging-in-Publication Data

Silverstein, Alvin.
    The tuberculosis update / Alvin and Virginia Silverstein,
and Laura Silverstein Nunn. — 1st ed.
       p. cm. — (Disease update)
    Includes bibliographical references and index.
    ISBN-10: 0-7660-2481-4 (hardcover)
       1. Tuberculosis—Juvenile literature. I. Silverstein, Virginia B.
II. Nunn, Laura Silverstein. III. Title. IV. Series.
RC312.S566 2005
616.9'95—dc22

                    2005005989

ISBN-13: 978-0-7660-2481-6

Printed in the United States of America

10 9 8 7 6 5 4 3 2

To Our Readers: We have done our best to make sure all Internet Addresses in this book were active and appropriate when we went to press. However, the author and the publisher have no control over and assume no liability for the material available on those Internet sites or on other Web sites they may link to. Any comments or suggestions can be sent by e-mail to comments@enslow.com or to the address on the back cover.

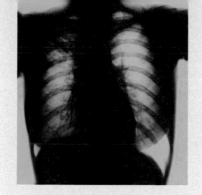

Contents

Tuberculosis

What is it?
A contagious disease caused by a bacterium; most commonly affects the lungs.

Who gets it?
People of all ages, all races, both sexes; high-risk groups include the elderly, young children, and those with weakened immune systems.

How do you get it?
Mainly by breathing air containing bacteria-contaminated droplets.

What are the symptoms?
Tiredness, lack of energy, weight loss, fever, night sweats, persistent cough, chest pain, blood in sputum.

How is it treated?
With antibiotics; curing tuberculosis (TB) may take nine months or more of continuous treatment; failure to complete treatment may result in a drug-resistant form of TB.

How can it be prevented?
Avoiding close contact with people with active TB; regular exercise, adequate sleep, and a good diet may help strengthen the body's defenses against developing active TB. BCG vaccine is used in most of the world, with varying results, but it is not used in the United States.

1

The Return of an Old Plague

TWENTY-YEAR-OLD SHI YALIN had been working hard for the last two years at a toy factory far from home. She worked to earn money to help her family back in Gulou Village in China. Lately, Shi had not been feeling well. She felt tired and run-down. She developed a bad cough that would not go away. Sometimes she even coughed up blood. She had very little appetite; in fact, she had lost more than twenty-two pounds in two months. She felt so ill that she finally went home to her village. If she rested for a while, she thought, she would get better. Maybe her mother's home cooking would help her get her appetite back.

Back in Gulou Village, however, Shi was not getting better. Finally she went to a local health center. A doctor there questioned her about her symptoms and gave her a complete physical examination. After taking an X-ray of her chest, the doctor told her that she had pulmonary tuberculosis (TB). The treatment, the doctor said, would be to stay isolated in a TB ward for two months while drugs brought the infection under control. Shi was scared to stay in a TB hospital and refused to follow the doctor's advice.

Two days later, a dedicated young French doctor, Sandra Deleule, visited Shi's home and changed her mind. Deleule was a volunteer working with Doctors Without Borders. This international organization provides emergency medical aid to people all over the world. Working with a local doctor and a translator, Deleule explained that Shi's illness could spread to other people. She was putting her family and other members of the village in danger. She was also risking her own life: If she did not get proper treatment, she could die. Doctors Without Borders would pay for Shi's treatment and the cost of her stay in the hospital. Shi reluctantly agreed. "I'm afraid to stay here," she commented after she arrived at the TB hospital. "But I'm afraid to make

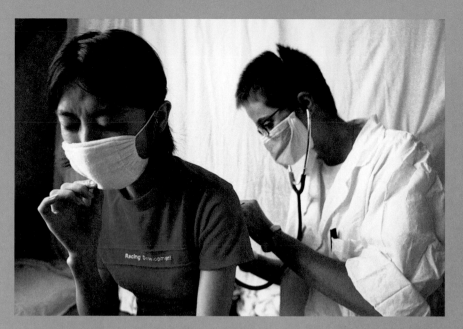

Dr. Sandra Deleule listens to twenty-year-old Shi Yalin's lungs after her arrival at the hospital. Shi has tuberculosis and decided to go to the hospital because she did not want to make her family sick.

my family sick, so I have to come here. It's my first time in a hospital."[1]

Shi and five other TB patients would be spending two months in the isolated TB ward. Then they would face six more months of treatment at home, getting weekly checkups by a local doctor.

Tuberculosis is commonly called TB. It is caused by a bacterium and mainly affects the lungs. This disease has been a serious health threat for thousands of years. It killed so many people during the Middle Ages (about A.D. 500 to 1500) that it was called the White Plague. TB has also been known as consumption because it

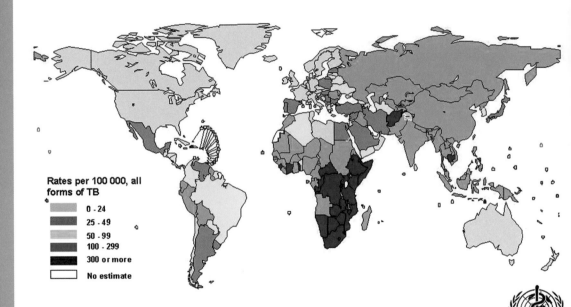

Estimated TB incidence rate, 2003

Rates per 100 000, all forms of TB

- 0 - 24
- 25 - 49
- 50 - 99
- 100 - 299
- 300 or more
- No estimate

The designations employed and the presentation of material on this map do not imply the expression of any opinion whatsoever on the part of the World Health Organization concerning the legal status of any country, territory, city or area or of its authorities, or concerning the delimitation of its frontiers or boundaries. White lines on maps represent approximate border lines for which there may not yet be full agreement.

©WHO 2004

This map shows the estimated number of TB cases throughout the world in 2003.

causes the body to gradually waste away and be "consumed."

In recent times, most people have gotten the idea that tuberculosis is a thing of the past. Powerful drugs, developed in the 1940s, had greatly reduced the number of TB cases in the United States and other developed countries. By the 1970s and 1980s, most Americans had practically forgotten about TB. As more nations became industrialized, better living conditions and improved methods of prevention, diagnosis, and treatment greatly reduced the number of people who got tuberculosis and the number who died from it. In fact, many doctors thought tuberculosis would soon be completely wiped out.

> Tuberculosis is still one of the world's biggest killers, especially in developing countries.

In most of the world, though, TB never really went away. It is still one of the world's biggest killers, especially in developing countries. Many countries in Latin America, Asia, the Middle East, and Africa are high-risk areas. Shi Yalin, for example, was one of an estimated 500 million people in China infected with the TB bacterium. Worldwide, around 2 billion people— one third of the world's population—are infected with the TB bacterium. And each year, 2 to 3 million people die of the disease.[2]

In the United States and other developed nations, TB made a sudden comeback in the mid-1980s, rising to a peak in 1993. Since then, the number of TB cases in the United States has been steadily decreasing, but this disease is still a public health concern. Some TB bacteria have changed into a kind of "superbug" that can no longer be killed by drugs that used to work. Today's tuberculosis is more difficult to stop, but it can be cured—as long as patients complete their treatment, which can take up to a year, and sometimes longer.

2

Tuberculosis Through the Ages

Y EARS AGO, IT WAS NOT UNCOMMON for tuberculosis to sweep through families. Sometimes it wiped out almost every member in the household. The Brontë family, for example, which included Charlotte and Emily Brontë, authors of the classic books *Jane Eyre* and *Wuthering Heights*, was devastated by the disease.

In 1820, Reverend Patrick Brontë moved his wife, Mary, and their six children to Haworth, England, to start his new job as clergyman at the Haworth Parsonage. The future seemed bright for the Brontës until the following year when Mary died of cancer. Mary's sister, Elizabeth Branwell, came to the parsonage to help take care of the children: five daughters, Maria, Elizabeth, Charlotte, Emily, and Anne, and the only son, Patrick Branwell (commonly called Branwell).

In 1824, the four eldest daughters were sent to a boarding school, where the conditions were harsh: Students lived in crowded, filthy rooms and were given very little food to eat. Soon an outbreak of illness swept through the school. Both Maria Brontë (age eleven) and her sister Elizabeth (age ten) died of tuberculosis. Charlotte was also very sick, and she and Emily were sent home to Haworth. The surviving siblings were heartbroken and soon formed very close relationships. Branwell and his sisters used their imaginations to make up stories about a set of wooden toy soldiers, plays they called the "Young Men."

By the 1840s, Charlotte, Emily, and Anne published a collection of poetry. Unfortunately, their book sold only two copies. In 1847, Charlotte's novel *Jane Eyre* was published and found immediate success. Around the same time, Emily's *Wuthering Heights* and Anne's *Agnes Grey* were also published. Branwell, who had failed as an artist, turned to alcohol and drugs. This took a toll on Branwell's body, and in September 1848, he died from tuberculosis. In December, Emily came down with

Anne, Emily, and Charlotte Brontë are shown in this group portrait. They died of tuberculosis, along with their sisters, Maria and Elizabeth, and their brother, Branwell. Branwell originally put himself in the portrait when he painted it, then decided to remove his image and painted over it. Now the paint is fading, and his image is starting to come through.

> Tuberculosis is more than just a couple of centuries old. It has been around for thousands of years.

tuberculosis and she, too, died. Emily never knew the success that her now-famous *Wuthering Heights* would achieve.

The devastating disease was not yet finished with the Brontës—the youngest sibling, Anne, died in May 1849, also from tuberculosis. Charlotte finally found happiness when she got married in 1854. Unfortunately, her happiness was short-lived—she died a year later, also of tuberculosis.[1]

An Age-Old Disease

The Brontës' health problems probably started when the four sisters were sent to boarding school. They lived in crowded, dirty surroundings. They were malnourished, which most likely weakened their body's defenses, making them vulnerable to tuberculosis.

Stories like those of the Brontë family were all too common during that time. But tuberculosis is more than just a couple of centuries old. It has been around for thousands of years. Scientists have found signs of tuberculosis in the spines of Egyptian mummies that date back to 4000 B.C.

The ancient Greeks called tuberculosis *phthisis,* from

Famous People Who Had Tuberculosis

Person	Year of Infection	Occupation
Rembrandt H. van Rijn	1669	Painter
Robert Burns	1796	Poet
John Keats (+ mother)	1821	Poet
Percy Bysshe Shelley	1822	Poet
Ludwig van Beethoven	1827	Composer
Frédéric Chopin	1849	Composer
Edgar Allan Poe (+ father, mother, wife)	1849	Writer
Charlotte Brontë (+ 4 sisters and 1 brother)	1855	Writer
Elizabeth Barrett Browning	1861	Writer
Robert Louis Stevenson	1894	Writer
Paul Gauguin	1903	Painter
Edvard Grieg	1907	Composer
Florence Nightingale	1910	Nurse
Alexander Graham Bell	1922	Inventor
Eleanor Roosevelt	1962	First Lady/ Diplomat
Vivien Leigh	1967	Actress
Cat Stevens (still living)	1968	Singer/musician

> As Europe became industrialized in the 1600s and 1700s, epidemics of TB occurred, infecting large numbers of people.

their word for "to waste away." Around 400 B.C., Greek physician Hippocrates described phthisis as the worst of all diseases at the time, and wrote that it was almost always fatal. He even warned other doctors not to visit patients in the late stages of the disease due to the danger of catching it themselves.

As Europe became industrialized in the 1600s and 1700s, epidemics of TB occurred, infecting large numbers of people. Franciscus Sylvius, a doctor in Holland, described structures that he called "tubercles" in a book that was published in 1679. Tubercles are small clumps of infected lung tissue typically found in TB patients. In the mid-1600s, TB caused one out of five deaths in London. In the 1700s and 1800s, one out of four European deaths was caused by TB. In America, too, tuberculosis ranked among the top deadly diseases.

Discovering the Cause of TB

Over 2,300 years ago, the famous Greek philosopher Aristotle said that tuberculosis could be spread from one person to another. He was right, but through the

Hippocrates, a Greek physician, wrote that tuberculosis (in his time called *phthisis*) was the worst of all diseases.

ages most people did not agree with this point of view. At various times it was believed that the disease was caused by an unhealthy climate, impure air, contaminated food, a tumor, mental depression, or damp soil; or that it was brought on by another disease such as typhoid fever or measles.

In 1720 English physician Benjamin Marten published *A New Theory of Consumptions*. This book suggested that TB was caused by "wonderfully minute creatures" and could spread to people who were exposed to an infected person for long periods of time. However, he believed, the disease rarely spread during short periods of contact.

One popular belief was that tuberculosis was inherited, especially since the disease often affected many members of the same family. Since a number of famous artists and writers died from tuberculosis, it was popularly believed in the 1800s that TB was an inherited trait that appeared in geniuses. It was also believed that the disease actually helped artists, writers, and musicians to think more clearly. Tuberculosis was often viewed as romantic or poetic, and it was glamorized in the arts and literature of the time. Tragic heroes and heroines died a brave, lingering death from the disease.

In 1865, Jean-Antoine Villemin, a French military surgeon, finally proved that TB was not inherited. He took pus and fluid from human TB patients and transferred the fluids to rabbits. Soon the rabbits developed tuberculosis. This showed that the disease could not be hereditary, since it could be passed from a human to a rabbit.

The cause of tuberculosis, a bacterium called *Mycobacterium tuberculosis,* was finally identified in 1882 by German physician Robert Koch.

The cause of tuberculosis was finally identified in 1882 by German physician Robert Koch. Koch discovered a staining technique that allowed him to see the tubercle bacillus (*Mycobacterium tuberculosis*), a rod-shaped bacterium that causes the disease. He found the organism in samples taken from eleven patients with severe TB, as well as from cattle, chickens, guinea pigs, monkeys, and rabbits. Koch's research also showed that TB is spread from person to person through contaminated droplets sprayed out into the air when an infected person coughs or sneezes.

Searching for a Cure

Even before Koch identified the cause of TB and how it is spread, people had all sorts of ideas on how TB should be treated—from breathing vapors from cow dung to drinking elephant blood. Since there was no real hope for TB patients at the time, the only thing doctors could recommend was plenty of rest and fresh air. As it turns out, this advice actually led to one of the first steps toward a cure. In 1854, Hermann Brehmer, a botany student who was suffering from TB, was told by his doctor to move to a healthier climate. Brehmer traveled to the Himalayas to continue his studies, and meanwhile searched for a cure. Surprisingly, he returned home cured of the disease. Brehmer decided to study medicine; eventually he became a doctor. In 1859, Brehmer opened the first sanatorium for TB patients, located in a pine forest in the mountains of Silesia in eastern Europe. The sanatorium was a live-in facility where patients could get plenty of fresh air, exercise, and a healthy diet.

The first TB sanatorium in the United States was

COVER UP!
YOUR COUGHS AND SNEEZES

Actual photograph of a sneeze

SPRAY SPREADS
COLDS · FLU · TUBERCULOSIS

THE ANNUAL SALE OF *Christmas Seals* MADE THIS POSTER POSSIBLE

In 1882, Robert Koch identified the bacteria that caused TB. People then knew that a cough or a sneeze could send hundreds of the bacteria into the air and could spread the disease. Messages to the public warned people about how TB is spread.

DENVER TUBERCULOSIS SOCIETY

DENVER TUBERCULOSIS SOCIETY

BE A GOOD FELLOW
DON'T SPIT ON THE STREETS

GOOD ROADS
ARE CLEAN
ROADS

opened in 1885 by Edward L. Trudeau in the Adirondack Mountains in New York. By the early 1900s, there were more than four hundred TB sanatoriums in the United States.

Were the sanatoriums really effective? Most likely. For one thing, isolating TB patients from the healthy population helped to reduce the spread of the disease. In addition, the daily dose of rest and good nutrition

Dr. Edward L. Trudeau opened the first TB sanatorium in the United States. This one-room cabin in Saranac Lake, New York, was known as "Little Red" and was built in 1884.

helped to strengthen patients' immune systems. As a result, many patients were cured. At the Trudeau sanatorium, 12,500 patients were treated during its seventy years of operation. When the Trudeau closed in 1954, 5,000 of those patients were still alive. By the 1950s, however, sanatoriums were no longer useful. Tuberculosis infections had been declining dramatically, not because of sanatoriums, but because of antibiotics.[2]

In the 1940s, researchers discovered antibiotics that were effective against tuberculosis. In 1944, the first TB drug, streptomycin, was given to a human patient. This patient, a twenty-one-year-old female with severe tuberculosis, was cured after four and a half months of receiving the drug. She later got married, had three children, and lived a long life.[3] Antibiotics had a huge impact on the downfall of tuberculosis. In 1952, isoniazid was added to the list of drugs against TB. This drug helped to reduce the TB rate even further. The number of active TB cases in the United States started declining by about 5 to 6 percent a year, from 84,304 cases in 1953 down to 22,201 cases in 1984—a 74 percent drop overall.[4]

Stamping Out TB

BUY
Christmas Seals
Fight Tuberculosis

One of the ways people collected money to stamp out TB was by using Christmas Seals. In 1907, American Red Cross volunteer Emily Bissell read an article about the special stamps being sold in Denmark to raise money to fight TB. Bissell used this idea to raise $3,000 for her local Delaware TB society. The following year, the Red Cross expanded Christmas Seals to a national effort, and it raised $135,000. In 1909, Christmas Seals sales raised $250,000. By 1929, sales had reached $5.5 million. By the early 1990s, Christmas Seals sales were close to $40 million each year—the largest nonprofit direct mail campaign in America.

Christmas Seals can now be ordered over the Internet, and designs can be personalized for individuals or local charitable groups.

The TB Comeback

As TB was on a steady decline, people were losing their fear of getting the disease. In 1989 the U.S. Department of Health and Human Services optimistically predicted that TB would be eliminated in the United States by the year 2010, affecting less than one case per one million people.[5]

> By the mid-1980s into the early 1990s, TB in the United States was not going away—it was making a comeback. Epidemics were spreading through prisons and hospitals like wildfire.

By the mid-1980s into the early 1990s, however, TB in the United States was not going away—it was making a comeback. From 1985 to 1992, the average number of TB cases per year grew from 22,201 to 26,673—a 20 percent increase. In New York City TB cases tripled, from the city's all-time low 1,307 cases in 1978 to 3,811 in 1992.[6] Epidemics were spreading through prisons and hospitals like wildfire.

What caused the sudden return of this age-old

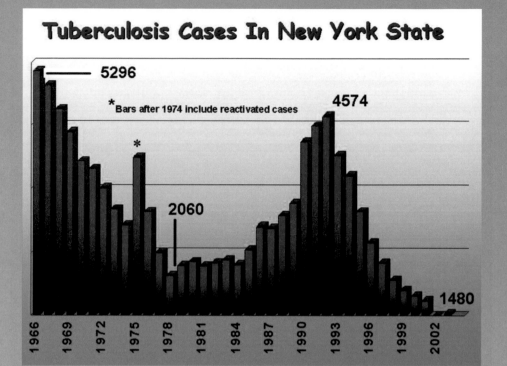

Tuberculosis Cases In New York State

5296

*Bars after 1974 include reactivated cases

4574

*

2060

1480

1966 1969 1972 1975 1978 1981 1984 1987 1990 1993 1996 1999 2002

Cases of tuberculosis in New York declined between 1964 and 1978. Then TB started to make a comeback, with cases peaking in 1992. Most of the cases occurred in New York City.

illness? A number of factors were involved. In the 1980s, there was an increase in drug abuse, homelessness, poverty, and the arrival of new immigrants from countries where TB is common. These factors combined to create ideal conditions for the spread of tuberculosis, since TB is often associated with poor hygiene and crowded living conditions.

The spread of AIDS has also helped to spread TB. AIDS is a disease caused by HIV, a virus that is passed through sexual contact and through the sharing of needles by users of injected drugs. People with AIDS are more vulnerable to other diseases—especially TB—because their immune systems are not strong enough to fight off germs. The rates of HIV infection are especially high among people in homeless shelters and prisons. TB bacteria can spread quickly under the crowded conditions that exist in those places.

Another reason for the TB comeback is that it is not just the "normal" kind of tuberculosis that is spreading. Some strains of tuberculosis have become drug resistant. That means that the bacteria have mutated (changed) and can no longer be killed by one or more types of antibiotics. Drug-resistant TB has become more and more common, making it more difficult to cure many of the new cases. In 1995, drug-resistant TB was reported in at least thirty-nine states.[7]

Thanks mostly to better control measures, TB in the United States has actually been declining since 1994. By the year 2004, the number of TB cases had dropped to 14,511 cases.[8]

TB Worldwide

In other countries around the world, encouraging progress has also been made—especially since 1993, when the World Health Organization (WHO) declared tuberculosis a "global emergency." In China, for example, which has the second highest number of TB cases, the TB rate dropped by about 30 percent in the decade from 1990 to 2000 and has continued to fall since then. China still has a long way to go, though. It still has 1.4 million new cases a year, and it is estimated that only about one third of all TB cases are detected.[9] Treatment programs are gradually covering more of the population so that more people can get medical help.

In India, which leads the world in TB cases, 400,000 die of TB each year. That is 20 percent of the 2 million TB deaths each year throughout the world. A major treatment program launched in 1997 is expanding rapidly. So far the program has been a success. In 2003, TB deaths in India had already been cut by one third, saving about 500 lives each day.[10]

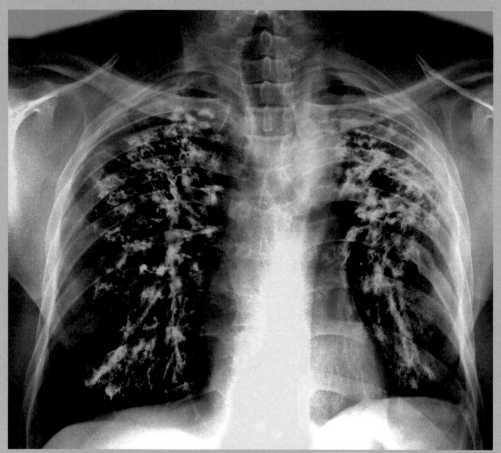

A colored chest X-ray shows scars (yellow) in the lungs of a tuberculosis patient. The heart is also shown, in red.

3

What Is Tuberculosis?

PHYLLIS WAS EIGHTY-NINE years old and battling a bad case of the flu. Just when she thought she was finally getting better, Phyllis started to feel ill again. She began to lose weight. She had a persistent cough and a fever as well. Her son was concerned and begged her to see the doctor, but she insisted that all she needed was some peace and quiet. Her condition did not improve, though, and she finally agreed to see a doctor.

X-rays showed that Phyllis had some fluid around her lungs, along with two tiny nodules (lumps) that were possible signs of long-healed tuberculosis lesions (sores). Fluid was then taken from the sac around the lungs. The laboratory results showed that tuberculosis bacteria were present. The doctor told Phyllis and her family that fortunately this was not a drug-resistant strain of TB. Therefore, antibiotics should kill all the bacteria. After eight months of drug treatment (consisting of a combination of the drugs rifampicin and isoniazid), Phyllis gained her weight and energy back, and she stayed healthy well into her nineties.

> More than 2 billion people around the world are infected with the TB bacterium, but only 10 percent of them will develop the disease.

Apparently, Phyllis had been infected with the tuberculosis bacterium many years before, when she was a child. She grew up in Brooklyn during a time when poor immigrants were coming to America in large numbers and there was a high rate of TB. For years, the TB bacterium remained hidden in her body without causing any harm. When Phyllis came down with the flu, the illness, combined with her advanced age, weakened her body's defenses (her immune system) so that the bacteria could come out of hiding and cause trouble.[1]

More than 2 billion people around the world are infected with the TB bacterium, but only 10 percent of them will develop the disease. In most cases, the immune system stops the bacteria from multiplying, and the disease does not get a chance to progress.

Of the unlucky 10 percent, though, about half of them will develop active TB (also called TB disease) soon after the infection or within a few years. People with active TB have symptoms and can spread the disease to other people. The other 5 percent may have latent TB: After the infection, the TB bacteria become dormant (inactive) inside the person's body but may be "reactivated" many years later. That is what happened to Phyllis. She had what health experts call reactivation TB.

What Causes TB?

Tuberculosis, or TB, is caused by several different kinds of bacteria that belong to a group called mycobacteria. Mycobacteria are microscopic rod-shaped organisms that measure from 0.5 to 4.0 microns (which is from about 1/50,000 to 1/6,000 of an inch). The bacteria that cause tuberculosis in humans are *Mycobacterium tuberculosis*. People can also get bovine TB, caused by *Mycobacterium bovis,* which infects cows.

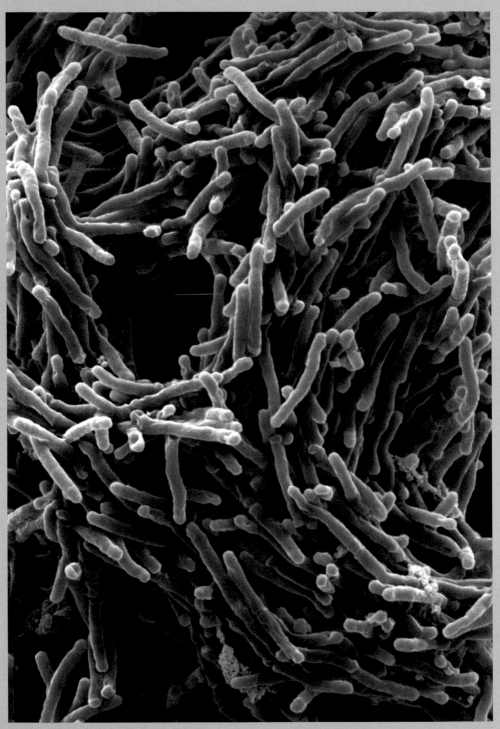

A microscope is used to view the *Mycobacterium tuberculosis* bacteria that cause tuberculosis. This image shows many of the rod-shaped bacteria.

Tuberculosis-causing bacteria are called tubercle bacilli. Tubercle bacilli do not grow in soil or water like some other bacteria. They must be passed from one human or animal to another. And they must have oxygen to live. Domestic animals such as pigs, rabbits, and chickens also get tuberculosis. The type that causes lung disease in chickens (*Mycobacterium avium*) does not usually affect humans, but for people with AIDS, it may be a serious problem. TB is not very common in wild animals and birds.

What Happens in the Body?

What happens when a person breathes in tubercle bacilli? In most cases, TB bacteria target the lungs. To understand what happens during a TB infection, you need to get an idea of how the lungs work.

When a person breathes, air is inhaled through the nose and mouth, passes down the throat (pharynx), through the voice box (the larynx), and continues down the main breathing tube, or trachea. Then the air flows through two large tubes (bronchi), which lead into the right and left lungs. The lungs are two large spongy organs that fit snugly on each side of the heart. The right lung is divided into three parts, or lobes. The left

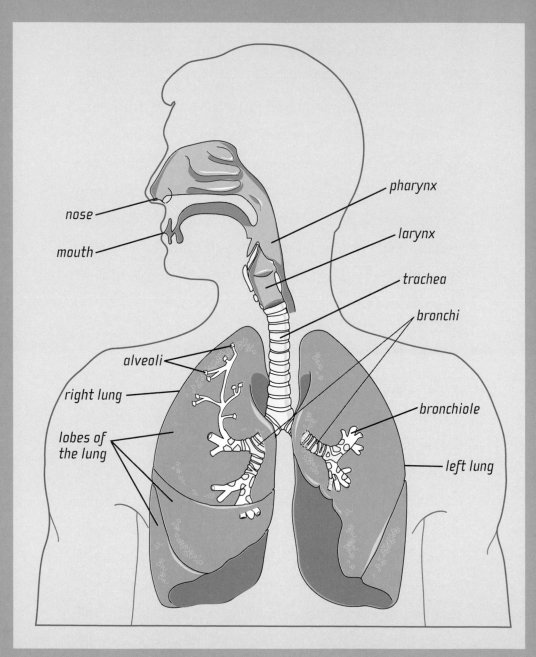

Air passes from the mouth or nose to the trachea, bronchi, and into the lungs. The air then travels into the smaller bronchioles and the tiny alveoli, where oxygen and carbon dioxide are exchanged between blood and air.

lung has only two lobes. (The left lung is smaller than the right because the heart is tipped toward the left and takes up more space on the left side of the chest.)

Inside the lungs, the bronchi branch into even smaller, almost threadlike tubes called bronchioles, which look like the branches of a tree. The bronchioles lead into millions of tiny balloon-like air sacs in the lungs called alveoli. Alveoli look like tiny bunches of grapes, but they are too small to see without a microscope. This is where the exchange of oxygen and carbon dioxide takes place.

Normally, it is not easy for TB bacteria to get past the body's defenses and travel down to the lungs. For example, if a person breathes in bacilli, some of the bacteria may be trapped by bristly hairs on the way into the nostrils. The germs that get past these hairs fall into a gooey fluid—mucus—that covers the lining of the nose. Mucus flows along the lining, carrying the trapped germs toward the back of the throat. Some lining cells are equipped with thin hairlike structures called cilia. Millions of cilia beat back and forth in a wavelike motion, up to 1,000 beats a minute, pushing mucus back up to the mouth. There the mucus can be coughed up, sneezed, or swallowed. (The combination of mucus and other substances coughed up from the lungs is called sputum.) Most bacteria that are swallowed are killed by the stomach acids.

If some of the tubercle bacilli do manage to get past the body's first line of defense in the airways, they will head deep into a person's lungs and hide out in the alveoli. Almost immediately, the body's immune system detects intruders. A team of powerful white-cell defenders, called macrophages, rushes to the scene. The macrophages try to gobble up the bacilli. Most other bacteria are easily broken down inside the macrophages, but TB bacteria are tough nuts to crack. They are protected by a thick waxy coating and are very hard to destroy. Some of the bacilli are able to survive and even continue multiplying inside the macrophages. Bacteria are usually easiest to kill while they are multiplying. TB bacteria multiply very slowly, though—once every 20 to 24 hours. (Most other bacteria multiply as often as every 20 to 40 *minutes!*) The slow reproduction of TB bacteria does not give the macrophages many chances to attack.

Bacilli-containing macrophages start to clump together inside the alveoli where the infection occurred. Other white blood cells, such as the T cells, join the clump to battle with the invaders. Within several weeks after the initial infection, the clumped cells will have formed a small, hard, gray swelling called a tubercle. (That is how the TB bacteria got their name.) The T cells produce chemicals that signal to the macrophages to kill TB bacilli or stop them from growing. These protective reactions also damage some of the lung cells.

The tubercle may gradually grow larger, destroying lung tissue around it. Soft, cheeselike areas are formed inside the tubercle as cells die. On the outside, tough scar tissue forms to surround the tubercle. The bacilli are trapped inside this wall of scar tissue, like prisoners in a jail cell. They are still alive, but they stop multiplying. People with this latent form of the disease do not usually show symptoms, and they are not contagious.

When the body's defenses are weakened, such as with HIV infection or in old age, the bacilli are able to break out of the tubercles and multiply. These reactivated bacteria invade the surrounding lung tissue and continue reproducing. More and more of the lung tissue is replaced by soft, cheeselike material, which may gradually become liquid. The liquid remains of the dead cells and bacteria are carried up the airways by the flow of mucus, leaving behind cavities (holes) and scar tissue. The lungs are literally being eaten away.

> Coughing is usually the first sign of TB, but in the early stages it is easy to mistake the disease for a bad cold that will not go away.

The buildup of mucus irritates the bronchi, causing coughing. At first this may occur only in the morning, because a pool of mucus forms deep in the lungs overnight. As the disease progresses, more mucus is formed, and coughing may occur all day long. Coughing is usually the first sign of TB, but in the early stages it is easy to mistake the disease for a bad cold that will not go away.

Eventually, tubercle bacilli may break through the walls of the alveoli and enter the tiny blood vessels that surround the air sacs. Blood begins to appear in the sputum that is coughed out. At first it may be just a slight pink stain, but later large amounts of blood may be coughed up. As more lung tissue is damaged, breathing becomes more difficult. There are fewer working alveoli to take in oxygen and send it to the body cells. Without enough oxygen, the cells cannot work effectively, and damage spreads through the body. The person feels tired and weak and loses weight. Tuberculosis can cause death quickly, but more often it is a long-term disease that gradually gets worse.

Kinds of TB

The most common type of TB is pulmonary tuberculosis, which affects the lungs. However, TB bacteria may be carried from damaged lung tissue through the bloodstream to other parts of the body. Almost any organ may be affected: the brain, bones and joints, skin, throat, intestines, liver, reproductive organs, kidneys, bladder, or lymph nodes.

Two of the most serious types of TB are miliary tuberculosis and tuberculosis meningitis. Miliary tuberculosis accounts for less than one percent of TB cases. Years ago, scientists thought that the small nodules that formed around tubercle bacilli looked like seeds of a kind of grain called millet. The Latin word for millet is *milium;* hence the term *miliary.* Miliary tuberculosis occurs when the infection spreads into the bloodstream. Without drugs, it is usually deadly. It used to be very common among children, but now it most often occurs among the elderly.

Tuberculosis meningitis used to occur mainly in children, but it, too, has become a disease of the elderly.

Before antibiotics were available, nearly all TB cases were fatal. Now four out of five patients are saved.

Unlike most types of TB, tuberculosis meningitis progresses very quickly. *Meningitis* means "inflammation (swelling) in the meninges," the coverings of the brain and spinal cord. Symptoms include headache, fever, and seizures; coma and death may occur without treatment. Before antibiotics were available, nearly all cases were fatal. Now four out of five patients are saved.

How Is TB Spread?

Tuberculosis is a contagious disease—it can be spread to other people. *Mycobacterium tuberculosis,* the TB bacterium that infects humans, can spread when a person with the disease coughs, sneezes, or even talks or spits, sending contaminated droplets into the air. These germ-filled droplets may be breathed in by nearby people. Tubercle bacilli can actually drift through the air like dust. And they can survive outside the body for weeks or even months—much longer than most other bacteria.

Mycobacterium bovis, which infects cows, can spread to people who eat food that is contaminated with the bacteria, or by drinking milk from cows with the disease. This form is highly rare in developed countries because milk is pasteurized (heated to kill bacteria), and cows are routinely tested for the disease.

Tuberculosis is more common in cities than in rural areas. The crowded conditions allow germs to spread easily. This railway station in India shows how crowded some places can be during the day.

TB is not as contagious as some other infectious diseases. It is unlikely for people to get TB through casual contact, such as being next to someone on the bus or in the supermarket. People with TB are more likely to spread the disease to people they spend time with every day. That is why TB tends to "run in families." TB rates are higher in cities than in rural

TB in the Air

Airplanes are famous for spreading germs. In an airplane, people breathe in air that other passengers breathed out. The air inside a plane in flight is constantly being recycled. Filters and other treatments help to clean out germs, but sometimes they are not good enough.

The first documented case of tuberculosis being spread on an airplane was reported in the spring of 1994. Normally, it takes days or weeks of exposure to TB germs for the disease to develop, but an eight-and-a-half-hour flight from Chicago to Honolulu was long enough for a woman with an active TB infection to spread the disease to four other passengers.[2] In 1998, the World Health Organization stated that people exposed to infectious tuberculosis on flights longer than eight hours had an increased risk of developing the disease.[3]

communities because crowded city conditions make it easier for the germs to spread. Rates of infection are particularly high in places where many people spend hours each day in close contact, such as in shelters, prisons, schools, nursing homes, and day care centers.

Who's at Risk?

Anyone can get TB, but there are certain groups of people that have a higher risk of getting the disease. People who spend a lot of time with these "risk groups" also have a greater risk for getting TB.

The groups at high risk include the following:

- People with HIV (the virus that causes AIDS) or other diseases that weaken the immune system
- People who are in close contact with those with active TB, such as family members or health care workers
- People from countries where TB is common, which include a number of countries in Latin America, Asia, the Middle East, and Africa
- Homeless people
- People in prisons
- People in nursing homes
- People who share needles to inject drugs

Carlos Guillen, a shortstop for the Seattle Mariners, had tuberculosis during the 2001 baseball season.

4

Diagnosing and Treating Tuberculosis

IN AUGUST 2001, Seattle Mariners shortstop Carlos Guillen started to feel wiped out during some of his games. Nearly every morning, he woke up drenched in sweat. His head was pounding, and he had a high fever. He also developed a fierce cough. This was one bad case of the flu, he thought.

Guillen loved playing baseball. At age twenty-five, he was happy just to be in the "big leagues." He was not going to let a little sickness keep him from playing ball. Every day he headed over to the ballpark, took a couple of pain relievers, and prayed he would magically feel better. But the illness would not go away—it just kept hanging on. Guillen was also getting nosebleeds, but he figured these were due to the collision he had recently had with a ballplayer from another team. Guillen's teammates knew he was not feeling well, but Guillen did not complain to his manager or his coaches.

Through September, Guillen's condition was getting worse. He started losing weight. He tried to eat, but he just did not have much of an appetite. He was coughing so much, his throat hurt. Then, on September 28, Guillen coughed up blood. He finally realized that this could be something serious. "I was coughing it up and it wouldn't stop," Guillen said, "so finally I checked myself into the hospital."[1]

The doctors at the hospital could not believe Guillen had continued playing baseball as long as he had. He was in really bad shape. After examining him and listening to him describe his symptoms, the doctors agreed that it sounded like a severe case of pulmonary tuberculosis. The diagnosis was confirmed by chest X-rays.

Everyone at the ball club was shocked at the diagnosis. After all, Guillen's TB skin test had come back negative in the team's routine medical screening during spring training. But according to health experts, the TB skin test is not always accurate. Many people test negative when they should test positive. Mitch Storey, the team doctor for the Seattle Mariners, told the press that it is possible that Guillen had been infected months before, when he was living in his native Venezuela (where TB is common) during the off-season.

At the hospital, Guillen was kept in isolation, since he was still contagious. He was given antibiotics right away. He needed surgery a few days later, though, to stop bleeding in one of his lungs.

In the meantime, Mariners manager Lou Piniella scheduled TB testing for more than sixty players, coaches, and front office personnel who worked closely with Guillen. As it turned out, two players, two coaches, and one clubhouse attendant tested positive for TB. Chest X-rays, though, showed that not one of them had the disease. This meant that they were not sick, but they had latent TB. They could develop the disease some time in the future. (But remember, most people with latent TB do not develop the disease.)

Just a few weeks after his antibiotics were started, Guillen was feeling better than he had in months. Even though he had missed the last nine games of the season, he was allowed to play in the playoffs and was almost back to his old self again. Meanwhile, he continued taking his medication for at least six months.

Tuberculosis is not always easy to identify. In fact, the disease is often mistaken for other illnesses, such as the flu, bronchitis, asthma, pneumonia, or just a bad cold. In many cases, people walk around sick for weeks or even months, hoping, like Carlos Guillen did, that the illness will just go away. But anybody who has a "cold" that does not seem to go away (longer than two weeks) or who notices strange or alarming symptoms, such as coughing up blood, should seek medical help.

Skin Tests

Most TB cases are first detected with a tuberculin skin test. This test shows whether a person has ever been infected by TB bacteria. When a person's body is

Symptom Checklist

People with active TB may have some or all of these symptoms:

- High fever
- A cough that will not go away
- Feeling tired all the time
- Weight loss
- Loss of appetite
- Coughing up blood
- Night sweats
- Difficulty breathing (later stages of TB)

exposed to TB bacteria, cells of the immune system learn to recognize and attack this particular kind of germ. Copies of the specialized immune cells remain in the body even after the battle is over. If the person is exposed to such bacteria again, these cells will be called into action.

> Tuberculosis is not always easy to identify. In fact, the disease is often mistaken for other illnesses, such as the flu, bronchitis, asthma, pneumonia, or just a bad cold.

The tuberculin skin test most widely used is the Mantoux test, also called the PPD (purified protein derivative) test. It is a sort of fake infection, in which a small amount of tuberculin (a protein from the tubercle bacillus) is injected under the skin of the forearm. The protein can fool the body's defenses, making it seem as though real TB bacteria are invading. If a person has been previously infected by tubercle bacilli, about two to three days later a red swelling will develop around the spot where the tuberculin was injected. A positive reaction to the test only shows that a person has been infected, not whether the bacterium is active. The test does *not* detect TB bacteria, just the presence of immune cells that are able to recognize them.

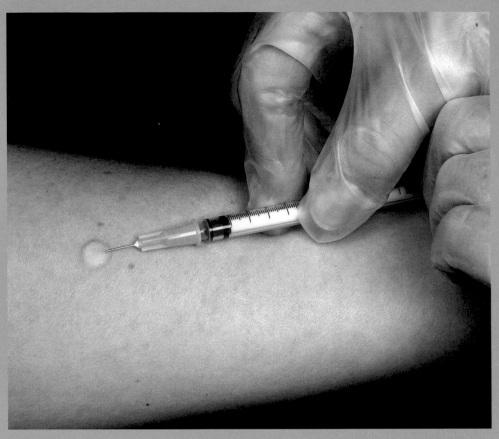

The Mantoux skin test is the most common test used to detect TB. A small amount of tuberculin is injected under the skin of the forearm.

The tuberculin skin test is a good diagnostic tool, but it is not always accurate. A person who has only recently been exposed to TB may not have a positive reaction for several weeks. It can take up to eight weeks for the body to build up immune defenses against the infection.[2] In such cases, the test result will be a false negative. The tuberculin test may give a false positive if a person has been exposed to a relative of the TB bacterium. In addition, a person whose immune system is damaged, such as someone with AIDS, may not have a positive skin test even when an active TB infection is present. This makes it especially difficult to diagnose tuberculosis in AIDS patients.

Chest X-Ray

The X-ray was first developed in 1895, but it was not available to the public until the 1930s. At that time, X-rays were used to screen large numbers of people for tuberculosis. Today X-rays are no longer used for routine screening, because having too many X-rays has

Trial and Error

Robert Koch, the physician who discovered tubercle bacilli in the 1880s, thought he had also discovered a cure for tuberculosis. He told the world of his "discovery," and doctors all over the world gave large doses of tuberculin to their TB patients. Unfortunately, this treatment made the condition worse, and many patients died as a result. It was a tragic mistake, but it yielded a useful diagnostic tool: the tuberculin test. Instead of using large doses of the substance, though, doctors now use a very small amount of tuberculin to detect TB infection.

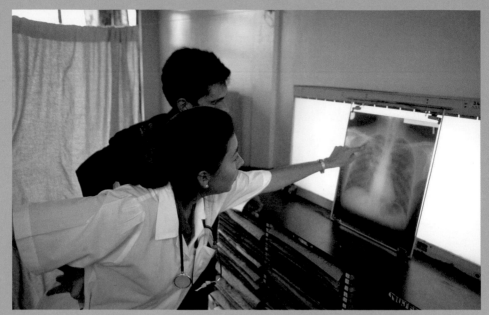
Dr. Veronica Arce points to a chest X-ray to show a TB patient the disease in his lungs.

been found to increase the chances of cancer. Now chest X-rays are usually taken only when a person has a positive tuberculin skin test.

A chest X-ray will show if there is an active infection, and if so, how much damage it has caused. In a chest X-ray, the doctor looks for tubercles or other signs of damage caused by tuberculosis in the lungs.

Laboratory Tests

Even an X-ray may not be able to detect tuberculosis. Sometimes it is hard to tell if lung damage was caused by TB or some other lung problem. Laboratory tests can detect the actual TB bacteria in sputum, blood, and other body substances. Samples of the fluid that cushions the brain and spinal cord may also be examined if TB meningitis is suspected.

In sputum tests, samples are treated with colored chemicals called stains. If particular bacteria are present, the stains produce a colored spot. However, these stains react not only to TB bacteria but also to some other kinds. The test may give false positive results if the person has another bacterial infection. Also, a negative result may not necessarily mean there are no

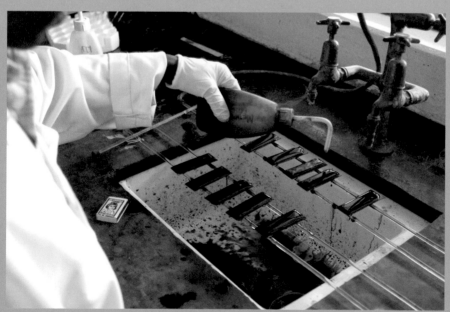

These slides contain sputum samples. They are being prepared for staining. The stains react to bacteria in the sample. This lab is the National TB and Leprosy Reference Laboratory in Uganda, Africa.

TB bacteria present. There may not be enough of the bacteria for the test to detect. In that case, the sample has to be cultured—grown in a laboratory under conditions that allow bacteria to multiply. When enough bacteria have grown, the technician can tell whether the bacteria are *Mycobacterium tuberculosis* or another kind of bacillus.

Tuberculosis can be cured with antibiotics, but treating it is a long process.

Laboratory tests can determine whether or not the bacteria are resistant to certain drugs, and therefore which drugs would be most effective for treatment. They can also give doctors an idea of how well the treatment is working. The acid-fast stain, for example, can indicate whether a patient needs to stay in isolation. Sputum samples are taken three days in a row, stained, and observed under a microscope. If TB bacilli are present, the test is positive, and the disease is still active. But if all three tests are negative, the patient is no longer infectious and can be let out of isolation.

Unfortunately, tubercle bacilli grow so slowly that laboratory tests usually take from two to eight weeks to determine whether the bacilli are present and from three to twelve weeks to test for effective antibiotics.

This can be a problem, since treatment should begin as soon as possible.

A more modern method, PCR (polymerase chain reaction), can give a TB diagnosis much faster than a culture—within twenty-four hours. Using PCR, a piece of the bacterium's DNA (the chemical carrying its hereditary information) is copied millions of times. This test can detect TB bacteria in a single infected lung cell among thousands of uninfected cells. But this high-tech test is too expensive to use for routine screening of the general public. It is used mainly as a follow-up test when doctors suspect a patient has TB.

Faster, more affordable tests are needed. The sooner a person receives a TB diagnosis, the sooner treatment can begin. These days, most normal TB cases—more than 90 percent—are cured when detected early. The death rate of untreated TB patients is around 40 to 60 percent.[3]

Treating TB Takes Time

Tuberculosis can be cured with antibiotics, but treating it is a long process—it can take months or even up to two years to kill the bacteria. Many other illnesses take only five to ten days to treat. The TB bacteria, with their tough waxy coats, are not easy to kill. They also grow very slowly, giving the drugs few chances to attack them while they are vulnerable.

Many TB patients have trouble handling the long treatment process. They may get tired of taking pills every day, or they may forget. Sometimes they stop

> One of the drawbacks of TB medication is that the drugs may have unpleasant side effects, such as headaches or nausea.

taking their medication because after a few weeks they start feeling better. Another drawback is that the drugs may have unpleasant side effects, such as headaches or nausea. However, when people do not complete their treatment—which, in most cases, is required for six to nine months—they can develop drug-resistant TB. This occurs when the drugs do not have enough time to kill *all* the bacteria. The "strong" ones survive and multiply, producing a whole population of drug-resistant bacteria. Soon the TB infection returns, and the person becomes sick again. This time, though, the drugs that were used before no longer work. Many people have developed multiple-drug-resistant (MDR) TB—the bacteria cannot be killed by two or more drugs. These people are especially difficult to treat.

Cases of drug-resistant TB have been rising dramatically since the 1990s. Doctors are now prescribing a combination of three or four drugs for most TB patients to prevent the development of drug-resistant TB. The most commonly used TB drugs are isoniazid, rifampicin, streptomycin, pyrazinamide, and ethambutol. The drugs must be taken every day for the treatment to work, even if the patient feels better. The idea is to kill *all* of the bacteria. When the treatment is completed, then the TB will not come back.

Can Surgery Help?

Before effective anti-TB drugs were discovered, surgery was used to treat many TB patients. Now that drug-resistant TB is becoming more common, doctors are forced to go back to some of the old surgical techniques—but only as a last resort.

One procedure, which was very popular in the past, is called pneumothorax. Air is pumped into the thorax, the chest cavity that surrounds the lungs. This causes the diseased lung to collapse, giving the lung a better chance to heal. Later the lung is allowed to reinflate so that the patient can breathe normally again.

Lung resection involves removing parts of the lungs that have been damaged. When the diseased parts have been removed, the remaining healthy parts can work normally.

Antibiotics are used to prevent infection that can develop after an operation.

In modern times, pneumothorax and lung resection have been used only to treat severe cases of tuberculosis.

5

Tuberculosis and Society

ALONZO MASSIE HAD BEEN BATTLING both tuberculosis and AIDS for more than two years. He could not seem to keep up with all the medicine he had to take, and now he felt as if the illnesses were finally winning. In April 1998, Alonzo walked into a New York City hospital hoping to get some medical help. Instead, the city hospital sent him to an isolation room at Bellevue Hospital because his condition was infectious, and he posed a public health threat. Alonzo was then sent for treatment at another New York hospital, called the Goldwater Memorial Hospital, on Roosevelt Island.[1]

Goldwater Memorial Hospital was no ordinary hospital. Patients there could take part in a number of activities, from exercise classes to sewing and horticultural groups, volleyball games, and watching television and movies. Besides the regular visits from the doctors treating their condition, patients could see dermatologists, dentists, counselors, and hairdressers. All this may sound like a day at the spa, but Goldwater was actually a detention center for TB patients who refused or were unable to complete their tuberculosis treatment. In 1993, when TB cases were getting out of

In 1993, the New York City Department of Health started sending patients to detention centers. Goldwater Memorial Hospital, shown here, housed and treated TB patients until 2001.

control, the New York City Department of Health was given the power to send TB patients to special detention centers against their will to complete their treatment.

At Goldwater, a guard watched the exit and common areas twenty-four hours a day. No one was allowed to go outside. Healthcare workers watched patients take their medicines every day. If the patients refused to take their medicine, they could be locked inside their rooms. Many patients complained that they felt like they were in jail. "Would you like to be inside for nine months with no fresh air?" asked Verena Fuller, one of the Goldwater patients.[2] Patients who objected to the detention were allowed a court hearing.

More than two years after he entered Goldwater, Alonzo Massie had taken his last TB medication and was allowed to leave the center and go back to "normal life." But Alonzo still had to take a whole different set of medications for his AIDS condition. This time, he promised, he would not miss a single dose, because he did not want to become resistant to the AIDS drugs as he had with tuberculosis.

Some medical experts believe that the fear of being locked up helped motivate many TB patients to cooperate with their treatment programs. By the time

Goldwater's detention ward closed in 2001, only about 220 patients had been treated there.[3] And no more than 47 patients had been detained at any one time in all of New York City.[4]

Is It Right to Lock Up Sick People?

We all know that anybody who breaks the law can be put in jail. But why are some TB patients treated like prisoners? For one thing, TB is not like the common cold, a mild sickness that will eventually go away. TB is a serious, life-threatening illness that can kill people when not treated properly. When people do not complete their treatment, for whatever reason—the side effects, they forget, or because it is a nuisance—they can

Who's to Blame?

It is easy to blame the spread of drug-resistant TB on patients who do not take their medicine. Some researchers say the focus should be on better drugs. Dr. Clifton E. Barry III, a researcher at the National Institute for Allergy and Infectious Disease, believes that stronger drugs would shorten the treatment period—to as little as two weeks. However, even though the U.S. government has taken a greater interest in TB since the early 1990s, health experts say there still is not enough money provided for TB drug research.[5]

put others at risk as well. This, in turn, can affect a whole community.

What should we do with people who refuse to take their medication? Some doctors believe that the only way to make sure these people follow treatment is to

> **Keeping patients on a treatment program until their treatment is finished helps ensure a full recovery.**

confine them. Others believe that this is a violation of people's rights. But what about the rights of the people who come in contact with them? How important are an individual's rights compared to the safety of society?

For years, our society has made it a practice to protect the community by isolating patients with serious infectious diseases. Many TB patients, however, are no longer infectious, yet they still have to be "locked up." This has stirred up a lot of controversy. In the past, patients were allowed to leave once they were no longer infectious. However, after they left, many patients stopped their treatment and later got sick again. Keeping patients on the program until their treatment is finished helps ensure a full recovery.

DOTS Worker Up Close

When Rebecca Stevens started her job as an outreach worker at the New Jersey Medical School National Tuberculosis Center in Newark, she looked very professional in her business suit and high heels. But this look lasted only three days. Stevens found out quickly that if she wanted to gain the trust of her patients—many of whom had problems with drugs and alcohol and lived in run-down apartments—she had to blend into the community. Now Stevens shows up to work in a pair of baggy pants, a faded T-shirt, and sneakers. This laid-back approach and her down-to-earth attitude have helped her become one of the most respected workers in the fight against TB.

As a fieldworker for the DOTS program, Stevens is in charge of ten to fifteen TB patients at a time. She visits each one five days a week and watches them take all of their pills on schedule. Sometimes the patients are not easy to find, or they may refuse treatment. If a patient refuses

Connecting the DOTS

Today, the main program recommended by the World Health Organization (WHO) for controlling TB is called DOTS (directly observed treatment, short-course). The DOTS program is a lot cheaper and less controversial than isolating TB patients in hospitals. In the DOTS program, TB patients are allowed to live their lives in the comfort of their own homes, but every day they are visited by a health care worker, who watches to open the door, Stevens will come back several times. She also questions friends and neighbors until she finally tracks down her patient. Then she tries to persuade him or her to return to treatment. This almost always works. Sometimes incentives help even more, such as five-dollar vouchers for local public transportation, five-dollar coupons for groceries, or cans of healthy drinks.

A patient who *still* refuses treatment may receive a stern letter from Newark's health department, stating that he or she must complete treatment for the safety of others. Usually this works. If it does not, however, the final step is getting a court order to have the person admitted to a hospital. This is very rare.

Rebecca Stevens seems to have a dangerous job. After all, she often visits places where many police officers would not go. But Stevens has developed a close, respectful relationship with the people in the community. She has made it a point not to judge them. She is there just to help them and the people close to them. And keeping them safe helps to keep others safe.[9]

them take all of their medication, in the right doses and at the right times.

Since it started in the early 1990s, the DOTS program has become one of the most successful TB control strategies. More than 110 countries now participate in the program. Worldwide, DOTS has a nearly 80 percent cure rate, and drug-resistant rates have dropped.

In India, the nation with the world's highest TB rate, about 728 million people participate in the DOTS program. The treatment success rate there has been over

Dr. Lee Reichman of the New Jersey Medical School National Tuberculosis Center supports programs that help patients take their tuberculosis medications. In the background, nurse Diana Ellis interviews a patient.

80 percent, a sharp increase from the roughly 30 percent with the old standard treatments.[6]

In China, which has the world's second largest TB rate, a survey conducted in 2000 concluded that the TB rate fell by 30 percent—about 382,000 cases—thanks to the DOTS program there.[7]

Generally, health officials believe that most people who stop treatment need incentives rather than detention. Most TB patients complete their treatment when health workers stay in touch with them or coax them to a clinic. This personal contact helps to form a connection between individual patients and health care workers. Sometimes, however, other incentives may also be needed. "If the public doesn't want drug-resistant TB, and if bribing people is the way to get them to take their medicine, then I say bribe them," says Lee Reichman, MD, head of the New Jersey Medical School Pulmonary Division.[8] Incentives can range from a free hot lunch to food coupons or store vouchers, or even money.

6

Preventing Tuberculosis

IN 1998, WHEN PEOPLE FOUND OUT that a fourteen-year-old girl from Clifton, New Jersey, had active tuberculosis, panic ran through the whole community. Some parents even suggested that local schools should be closed. The high school she attended held a meeting to calm the parents. Health officials assured them that TB is very curable and that it is rarely fatal in this country.

In the meantime, 163 people at Clifton High School were screened for TB. Test results showed that 46 students were infected, but none of them had the disease. Even though they were not infectious, the students who tested positive for the bacterium were treated with isoniazid for a period of six to twelve months. This would kill the TB bacteria in their body so that they would not become infectious sometime in the future.

Many Americans are shocked when they hear that TB is in their community. They feel that this is something that happens in other countries, not in the United States. As we now know, that is not true. "TB is out there—it's everywhere in the world," says TB expert Lee Reichman. "We see far less of it in the U.S. because we have such effective prevention and treatment programs."[1]

Prevention is the key. If we can stop TB from spreading, we can someday stop TB altogether.

> "TB is out there—it's everywhere in the world."
> — Dr. Lee Reichman

A Vaccine for TB

The best way to prevent any contagious disease is to develop a vaccine for it. A vaccine causes the immune system to make antibodies that can attack the germ. If the disease germ later invades the body, these antibodies can be used as a pattern for mass-producing enough to defend against the invaders. People who receive a vaccine build up an immunity against the disease. They will not get the disease if they are exposed to the germs that cause it.

The TB vaccine most widely used was developed by two French scientists, Albert Calmette and Camille Guérin and first became available to the public in 1921. The vaccine, known as Bacille Calmette-Guérin (*bacille* is French for *bacillus*), or BCG for short, contains a live, weakened form of the TB bacterium that causes TB in cattle.

BCG is widely used around the world, especially where TB is common. Billions of people have been vaccinated. However, it is not widely used in the United States. Part of the reason is that no one really knows how well it works, or if it does at all. Studies done on the effectiveness of the vaccine have given greatly varying results in different parts of the world, from 80 percent protection in some areas to no protection in others.[2] However, the vaccine does seem to provide some protection to young children against TB complications, such as meningitis. Therefore, the World Health Organization (WHO) recommends the vaccine for newborns in developing countries and other TB hot spots. Since TB is not as common in the United States as it is in other parts of the world, health experts do

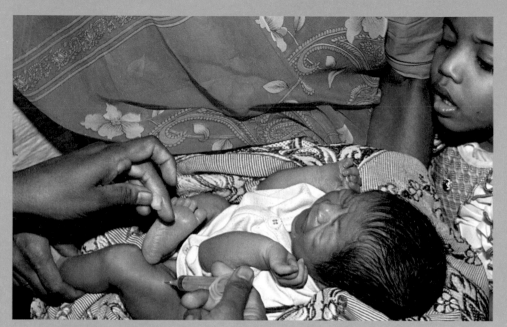

In countries where TB is a problem, newborns are vaccinated against the disease.

not think widespread vaccination with such limited protection is worthwhile in the United States.

Another reason the vaccine is not used in the United States is that people who receive it may test positive on skin tests, even if they do not have the disease. Doctors in the United States could lose skin tests as a valuable diagnostic tool.

Screening for TB

It was not too long ago that all American schoolchildren were routinely tested for TB. As TB became less of a public threat, these testing programs stopped. Sometimes widespread screening is necessary, though, when active TB outbreaks appear, such as the one in Clifton, New Jersey.

Generally, the Centers for Disease Control and Prevention (CDC) recommends routine TB screening for high-risk groups. These groups include the following:

- People in close contact with a person with infectious TB (such as those living in the same household)
- People with HIV or AIDS
- People who share needles to inject drugs
- People from areas where TB is common (such as many countries in Asia, Africa, and Latin America)
- Health care workers
- Homeless people
- People in nursing homes or mental institutions
- People in prisons

What Can You Do?

You can help in the fight against TB. For one thing, stay away from anyone you know who has infectious TB, and keep your distance from people who are constantly coughing. These measures can help reduce the risk of spreading TB.

The CDC recommends that people at high risk of contracting TB, such as the homeless, get routine screening.

HIV infection and AIDS have been important factors in the spread of TB, so you can also fight against TB by avoiding AIDS. Protect yourself by not using illegal drugs and not having unprotected sex. Both of these are risky behaviors that can lead to HIV infection. Remember, HIV weakens the body's defenses and helps TB germs to survive and multiply.

Living a healthy lifestyle can also help to keep the body strong and fit. Make sure you get enough sleep and exercise, and eat the right foods. Remember, TB attacks people when their bodies are weak and vulnerable. A strong, healthy immune system will have a better chance of fighting off TB bacteria.

7

Tuberculosis and the Future

IN 1996, CAROL NACY, a longtime researcher in the field of microbiology, immunology, and infectious diseases, was surprised when the National Institutes of Health asked her to look into funding for future TB research projects. The truth was, Nacy had no idea that TB was still a problem: "I never paid much attention to TB. I was one of the vast number of people in the United States who 'knew' we had cured TB worldwide."[1] Soon Nacy learned the truth about TB from other scientists working in the field. She could not believe what she heard. "I heard these outrageous statistics. The number of young people infected! The number one killer of women, more than

Carol Nacy started the Sequella Global TB Foundation.

any problem of pregnancy and childbirth! I was outraged by that. The number one killer of people with HIV. Number two killer of men. I realized how many people are dying of TB. We hadn't cured TB. We hadn't cured TB in the United States, and we certainly hadn't touched it abroad."[2]

This was a real eye-opener for Carol Nacy, who decided to dedicate her future to TB research and the development of new diagnostic tools, drugs, and especially vaccines. In 1997, Nacy used her own money to start up the Sequella Global TB Foundation to achieve her goals.

Several of the foundation's lines of research have proved fruitful, producing new TB tests and several vaccines that may be more effective than BCG. Clinical trials of one vaccine began in 2004. The work of the foundation, now called Aeras Global TB Vaccine Foundation, was considered so promising that in February 2004, the Bill and Melinda Gates Foundation donated $82.9 million to help fund the work. This more than doubled the amount of money available for TB research.

TB research has been making exciting progress. It has focused on several main areas, such as developing better tests, finding better treatments, and developing vaccines to prevent TB and even to treat people who have already been infected with the TB bacterium. The tremendous progress in genome research, discovering the hereditary instructions for many organisms from bacteria to humans, has been a tremendous aid in the progress of TB research.

The Genome Revolution

Genes are found in all living organisms. They are the chemical blueprints that make you who you are. Your genes determine the color of your eyes and hair and the shape of your nose. They also instruct your body to produce enzymes, proteins that help the body function. The genes of bacteria contain instructions for their size and shape, what kinds of cells they infect, and how deadly they are.

In 1998, scientists working for the Human Genome Project successfully decoded the entire genome (genetic sequence) of the tuberculosis bacterium. In 2000, researchers announced that they had worked out the complete sequence of the human genome. Genes determine how a bacterium attacks its host. They also determine which people are more vulnerable to the

When Accidents Happen

In December 2003, researchers at the University of California, Berkeley thought it was safe to assume that disabling a gene with the potential to be deadly would make the organism harmless. What happened was not what they expected. After disabling a set of genes in a strain of TB bacteria, the researchers were shocked to discover that the bacteria had mutated into a form that multiplied more quickly and was *more* deadly than the original. Critics of gene technology worry that this kind of mistake could be disastrous if such a mutant got out into the community, creating a whole new public health threat.[3]

attack and how effectively the body can defend itself. Knowledge of the bacterial and human genomes can lead to the development of new, more effective drugs and vaccines.

Scientists have made tremendous medical advances using gene technology. Once they can figure out what certain genes do, they can even change a bacterium's genes so that it will no longer cause any harm.

New Vaccines

In 2004, the first human testing of two new TB vaccines began. One was sponsored by the Aeras Foundation and the other by the National Institutes of Health. Both of them are recombinant vaccines, made using modern DNA technology.

Recombinant vaccines are made by a technique called gene splicing. Researchers use special enzymes that act as "chemical scissors" to cut apart the DNA from microorganisms, such as the TB bacillus. They can cut out the gene for making a particular protein. Then, using other enzymes that act as a kind of "chemical glue," they splice (join) the gene into the DNA of a different organism. In this case, researchers spliced a piece of DNA from the TB bacillus into the bacterium used for the BCG vaccine. When this recombinant BCG is introduced into a person's body, it stimulates the production of antibodies. Some of the antibodies match up with BCG proteins, while others are a match for the TB protein that was spliced in. If a person is then infected by TB bacteria, there will be a pattern on file for producing antibodies specifically targeted against the TB germs. Thus, the recombinant vaccine is much better than BCG in protecting people from tuberculosis. By using recombinant vaccines, scientists hope to produce effective protection without the danger of actually causing the disease. The vaccine contains only a small part of the TB bacterium (the genes for only one or two proteins), rather than a whole live disease germ.

One of the vaccines, supported by Aeras, contains a gene for one TB protein. The other experimental vaccine, developed under the sponsorship of the National Institutes of Health, contains the genes for two different TB proteins. It has been a long road just to get

> More years of human testing will be needed before the recombinant vaccines against tuberculosis are ready for general use.

to this point. Both vaccines have gone through years of development, from the test tube through animal studies. More years of human testing will be needed before the vaccines are ready for general use. The Aeras vaccine, for example, began phase I testing in 2004; the vaccine was given to a small number of volunteers to determine if the vaccine is safe and what the best doses are. Any vaccine must go through two more phases of human testing, involving larger and larger numbers of volunteers, to determine if it actually prevents the disease. The Aeras Foundation had hoped the vaccine would be ready for Phase III testing by 2007. Even if those tests are successful, it will take another year or two to evaluate the results and get the vaccine ready for sale.[4]

Better Diagnostic Tests

In the meantime, it is important to work with the TB cases we have now. If TB cases can be diagnosed earlier, they will be easier to treat. Researchers are working on some new diagnostic tests that look promising. These tests can give results in one to two days, so treatment can start quickly. One is a breath test, similar to the Breathalyzer that police officers use to measure the amount of alcohol in a person's blood. In the case of TB, a doctor can use this "electronic nose" to scan for patterns of odor chemicals that appear when TB bacteria are present. Scientists have recorded the "odor fingerprints" of hundreds of organisms, each of which produces distinct chemicals that are found in the waste products it leaves in the bloodstream.[5]

Another test uses the same chemicals that produce a firefly's glow to determine which drugs can kill the

The large machine on this lab desk is an "electronic nose." The machine reads a patient's breath to detect odors due to the presence of tuberculosis bacteria. This machine is used for a wide range of applications in the medical and food industries.

TB strain a patient has. This test gives results in just 24 to 48 hours.

Researchers are also excited about a new skin test called the Transdermal Patch for Active TB. Unlike the widely used Mantoux test, the transdermal patch can actually distinguish between active TB and latent TB. The patch, which is placed directly on the skin like a Band-Aid, responds to a protein found only in mycobacteria that cause TB in humans. It will not test positive in people who have received the BCG vaccine, or those who are infected with other mycobacteria. It also will not test positive in people who recently finished TB treatment.[6]

Better Treatments

The most recent drug approved for TB treatment was rifampicin, back in 1971. For a long time, drug researchers did not bother to look for new TB drugs. They figured that with a number of effective antibiotics already available, no more were needed. Then drug resistance began to appear and spread among TB patients. Doctors found that using just one or two of the old drugs was not good enough. They had to use a multiple drug approach—and in a few cases, all the drugs they had could not save patients with multiple-drug-resistant TB. New drugs, with different ways of attacking the TB germs, are needed.

Researchers today are using several approaches in the search for new TB drugs. Some groups are looking at chemicals that drug companies discovered years ago but never developed. They thought at the time that there were already enough TB drugs on the market.

A major drug company has recently screened a million different chemicals for activity against TB bacteria. Many of them showed good results in a culture dish. Now the company is determining which ones are the best prospects for new TB drugs.[7] Other research groups are finding promising new drugs in the chemicals produced by plants.

Since the early 1990s, a lot has been discovered about exactly how the various types of drugs attack TB bacteria, and how the germs become resistant to drugs. Mutations (changes) in key genes can make a bacterium able to survive in spite of high doses of a drug that would kill most TB germs. A gene involved in resistance to TB drugs was identified in 1992; by 2000, scientists had already found ten different gene mutations for TB drug resistance. In 1992, researchers also figured out exactly how the drug isoniazid works (it prevents the bacteria from building their tough outer covering). Soon they learned that some other TB drugs work by stopping the bacteria from making proteins or DNA. This knowledge is helping in the search for better treatments.

A new drug called PA-824 seems very promising. It belongs to a different chemical family than previous

Better Than DOTS?

Sequella, Inc., has come up with a clever device that could help patients cooperate better in their treatment. It is a wristwatch that can monitor the presence of TB drugs in a patient's blood. Researchers have combined TB drugs with a fluorescent chemical. The combined drug has a green glow that can be picked up by the wristwatch detector from the blood flowing through tiny blood vessels close to the surface of the skin. This device could reduce the need for people to sit with patients and watch while they swallow each dose. Instead, health workers can tell if a patient took his or her medicine by checking the record in the wristwatch.

Oddly enough, says Sequella's Carol Nacy, doctors treating conditions such as alcoholism and bipolar depression seem more enthusiastic about the wristwatch detector than people working with TB patients. "The tuberculosis people say, 'We know DOTS, and it works.' But the cost of one health worker monitoring six patients can pay for 500 of these monitors, which will be priced at less than $30 each." A patient who completes the treatment successfully gets to keep the watch. This can be a valuable prize for someone in a developing country.[8]

drugs, so the TB bacteria are not likely to be resistant to it. The Global Alliance for TB Drug Development has formed a partnership with a drug company, Chiron Corporation, to bring the drug through the necessary testing on human volunteers and TB patients.[9]

Meanwhile, in December 2004, Johnson and Johnson Pharmaceutical researchers announced the discovery of another new antibiotic, R207910, that was ready for clinical trials in human patients. In experiments on mice with TB, when given together with other TB drugs, R207910 cut the treatment times in half. The new antibiotic also did not have unpleasant side effects in tests on healthy human volunteers. The research team discovered that R207910 stops a key step in the TB bacterium's production of energy to power its activities. No other antibiotics known work in this way. If it is just as effective in humans as it is in mice, the new drug will not only shorten TB treatment but also lessen the chances of drug resistance.[10]

Some researchers believe that an effective TB vaccine could also be used as a treatment for people who are already infected. It would stimulate the body to produce germ-fighting antibodies that would go into action as soon as any latent TB bacteria start to break out of the tubercles. Reactivation could thus be prevented by taking a single dose of the vaccine, instead of months of treatment with drugs that might have side effects. Scientists do not know if the vaccination would provide lifelong protection, or if periodic booster doses would be needed. Either way, it would be a lot easier to take, and a lot cheaper, than drug treatments. These advantages would be especially important in developing countries, where resources of money and trained health workers are very limited.

TB control efforts—from programs ensuring patients complete their treatment to avid research on new TB tests, treatments, and promising vaccines— have kept the TB rate on a steady decline since 1994. Researchers are on the right track, and in time, there should be an effective TB vaccine that will someday wipe out tuberculosis from all parts of the world.

Questions and Answers

I thought TB was something that people used to get in the old days. Why is it in the news now? By the mid-1980s, TB was thought to be cured in the United States. In 1985, however, the number of TB cases started to increase again. The growing numbers of HIV-infected people and homeless people provided the perfect conditions for TB to spread. Efforts to control the TB problem were slow because most of the health care services for TB patients had been closed down. In developing countries, TB never stopped being a big problem; today, it is a top infectious-disease killer worldwide.

Can I catch TB by sharing a drink with someone who has the disease? Probably not. TB is spread mainly by breathing in air containing bacteria-carrying droplets coughed or sneezed out by someone with TB.

A kid in my class is constantly coughing. Could he have TB? Coughing may be a telltale sign of TB, but it can also be caused by a number of other health problems, such as a bad cold, allergies, asthma, or pneumonia. The best way to find out if you have TB is to get a tuberculin skin test.

If it turns out that the kid in my class does have TB, could I get it too? Possibly. TB can be spread through repeated exposure to a person with the active disease. If you sit near an infectious person every single day, you and your classmates are at risk for developing the disease.

My tuberculin skin test just came back positive. Does that mean that I'm going to get sick? Not necessarily. The positive test may mean that you are carrying the TB bacterium but don't have the active disease. There is a chance that you could develop an active case of TB sometime in the future. Most people carrying the bacterium—about 90 percent—never go on to develop the disease.

Why do some people with a positive skin test get treated with a drug even if they're not sick? Doctors may treat latent TB with isoniazid or a combination of drugs to kill the TB bacteria, which in turn, will prevent an infection from developing into the disease.

If there's a vaccine to prevent TB, why isn't it used in the United States? Studies show that the BCG vaccine may not be effective in preventing TB. And once you receive it, you may have a positive skin test—so it will be harder to diagnose TB if you do get the disease later on.

Why does TB treatment take so long? Usually when I get a bacterial infection, I have to take medicine for no more than ten days. The TB bacillus is not easy to kill. Antibiotics help to make it more vulnerable, but it takes time to wipe out all the bacteria. If the treatment is stopped too soon, some TB bacilli will survive and may later spread through the body. The germs that survive are more likely to be drug-resistant and therefore harder to treat.

Will we ever see a world without TB? Perhaps. Scientists are working hard to create promising new vaccines that are expected to be more effective than BCG. Unfortunately, it takes time before a vaccine can become widely available to the public. In the meantime, TB control programs are helping to decrease the number of TB cases worldwide.

TB Timeline

4000 B.C. ···· Signs of TB are left in the spines of Egyptian mummies.

About 400 B.C. ···· Hippocrates describes phthisis (Greek for "to waste away") as the worst of all diseases at the time.

300s B.C. ···· Aristotle claims TB is contagious.

A.D. 1679 ······· Book by Franciscus Sylvius describes lung nodules as tubercles.

1720 ······· Benjamin Marten suggests that TB is spread through prolonged exposure.

1840 ······· The word *tuberculosis* is first used.

1859 ······· Hermann Brehmer opens the first TB sanatorium.

1865 ······· Jean-Antoine Villemin proves TB is contagious.

1882 ······· Robert Koch discovers tubercle bacillus.

1885 ······· Edward L. Trudeau opens the first TB sanatorium in the United States.

1921 ······· BCG vaccine is used to prevent TB.

1944 ···· Streptomycin, the first effective antibiotic for TB, is discovered.

1952 ···· Isoniazid, one of the most important TB medications, is developed.

1986 ···· TB's downward trend in the United States reverses.

1992 ···· Researchers discover how isoniazid works against TB bacteria;
The first mutant gene that produces antibiotic resistance is discovered.

1993 ···· The WHO declares tuberculosis "a global emergency."

1994 ···· The TB rate in the United States begins to fall again. The genes of the TB bacterium are decoded.

For More Information

American Lung Association
1740 Broadway
New York, NY 10019
1-800-LUNG-USA (1-800-586-4872)
http://www.lungusa.org

Centers for Disease Control and Prevention
Division of Tuberculosis Elimination
1600 Clifton Road, NE
Atlanta, GA 30333
404-639-3534
Toll free: 1-800-311-3435
http://www.cdc.gov/nchstp/tb/

Global Alliance for TB Drug Development
59 John Street, Suite 800
New York, NY 10038
212-227-7540
http://www.tballiance.org

National Institute of Allergy and Infectious Diseases
6610 Rockledge Drive, MSC 6612
Bethesda, MD 20892-6612
http://www3.niaid.nih.gov

New Jersey Medical School
Global Tuberculosis Institute
UMDNJ
225 Warren Street, Second Floor East Wing
Newark, NJ 07103-3620
973-972-3270
Toll-free: 1-800-4TB-DOCS (1-800-482-3627)
http://www.umdnj.edu/globaltb/start.html

Chapter Notes

Chapter 1. The Return of an Old Plague

1. Greg Baker, "Up to 500 million Chinese believed infected with Tuberculosis," *Portsmouth Herald*, October 8, 2000, <http://www.seacoastonline.com/2000news/10_8_w1.htm> (January 11, 2005).

2. National Institute of Allergy and Infectious Diseases, "Tuberculosis," *NIAID Fact Sheet*, March 2002, <http://www.niaid.nih.gov/factsheets/tb.htm> (January 11, 2005).

Chapter 2. Tuberculosis Through the Ages

1. Eleanor Hubbard, "ClassicNotes: Emily Brontë," *GradeSaver.com*, March 5, 2000, <http://www.gradesaver.com/ClassicNotes/Authors/about_emily_bronte.html> (January 11, 2005); "Charlotte Brontë," <http://www.geocities.com/starrbright34/char.html> (January 11, 2005).

2. Barry E. Zimmerman and David J. Zimmerman, *Killer Germs* (Chicago: Contemporary Books, 1996), p. 75

3. Ibid., p. 78.

4. Carolyn Newbergh, "Tuberculosis: Old Disease, New Challenge," *The Robert Wood Johnson Foundation Anthology*, 2002, <http://www.rwjf.org/publications/publicationsPdfs/anthology2002/chapter_02.html> (January 11, 2005).

5. Ibid.

6. Ibid.

7. National Institutes of Health (NIH), National Institute of Allergy and Infectious Diseases (NIAID), "Tuberculosis," *NIAID Fact Sheet*, March 1997, <http://www.healthieryou. com/tb.html> (January 11, 2005).

8. Centers for Disease Control and Prevention, "Trends in Tuberculosis—United States, 2004," *MMWR Weekly*, March 18, 2005, <http://www.cdc.gov/mmwr/ preview/mmwrhtml/mm5410a2.htm> (August 3, 2005).

9. "TB Prevalence Rates in China Fall 30% Following Introduction of the DOTS Strategy," Press Release, *World Health Organization Western Pacific Region*, July 30, 2004, <http://www.wpro.who.int/public/press_ release/press_view.asp?id=407&tbp> (January 11, 2005).

10. The World Bank Group, "Tuberculosis Control Project," March 2004, <http://www.worldbank.org.in/ WBSITE/EXTERNAL/COUNTRIES/SOUTHASI-AEXT/INDIAEXTN/0,,contentMDK%3A20189356~pa gePK%3A141137~piPK%3A217854~theSitePK%3A29 5584,00.html> (January 11, 2005); The World Bank Group, "Indian Success in Tuberculosis Control Efforts," May 21, 2004, <http://www.worldbank.org.in/ WBSITE/EXTERNAL/COUNTRIES/SOUTHASI-AEXT/INDIAEXTN/0,,contentMDK%3A20208361~m enuPK%3A295605~pagePK%3A141137~piPK%3A141 127~theSitePK%3A295584,00.html> (August 3, 2005).

Chapter 3. What Is Tuberculosis?

1. Philip M. Tierno, Jr., *The Secret Life of Germs* (New York: Pocket Books, 2001), pp. 161–162.

2. Barry E. Zimmerman and David J. Zimmerman, *Killer Germs* (Chicago: Contemporary Books, 2003), p. 68.

3. Lee B. Reichman and Janice Hopkins Tanne, *Timebomb: The Global Epidemic of Multi-Drug-Resistant Tuberculosis* (New York: McGraw-Hill, 2001), p. 6.

Chapter 4. Diagnosing and Treating Tuberculosis

1. Chris Colston, "Mariners shortstop shakes off TB," *USA TODAY Baseball Weekly*, October 23, 2001, <http://www.usatoday.com/sports/bbw/2001-10-24/2001-10-24-guillen.htm> (January 11, 2005).

2. WrongDiagnosis.com, "Diagnostic Tests for Tuberculosis," June 23, 2003, <http://www.wrongdiagnosis.com/t/tuberculosis/tests.htm> (January 11, 2005).

3. Ibid.

Chapter 5. Tuberculosis and Society

1. Heather Vogell, "The Old Remedy," *Gotham Gazette*, <http://www.gothamgazette.com/commentary/43.vogell.shtml> (January 11, 2005).

2. Mireya Navarro, "Confining Tuberculosis Patients: Weighing Rights vs. Health Risks," *New York Times*, November 21, 1993, p. 45.

3. Roberto Acevedo, Ruth Wangerin, and Loretta Bennett, "Highlights from State and Local Programs," *TB Notes Newsletter*, CDC: Division of Tuberculosis

Elimination, No. 2, 2002, <http://www.cdc.gov/nchstp/tb/notes/TBN_2_02/highlights.htm> (January 11, 2005).

4. Lee B. Reichman and Janice Hopkins Tanne, *Timebomb: The Global Epidemic of Multi-Drug-Resistant Tuberculosis* (New York: McGraw-Hill, 2001), p. 149.

5. Vogell.

6. The World Bank Group, "Tuberculosis Control Project," March 2004, <http://www.worldbank.org.in/WBSITE/EXTERNAL/COUNTRIES/SOUTHASIAEXT/INDIAEXTN/0,,contentMDK:20189356~pagePK:141137~piPK:217854~theSitePK:295584,00.html> (January 11, 2005).

7. "TB Prevalence Rates in China Fall 30% Following Introduction of the DOTS Strategy," Press Release, *World Health Organization Western Pacific Region*, July 30, 2004, <http://www. wpro.who.int/public/press_release/press_view.asp?id=407&tbp> (January 11, 2005).

8. Geoffrey Cowley, "Tuberculosis: A Deadly Return," *Newsweek*, March 16, 1992, p. 57.

9. Reichman and Tanne, pp. 155–161.

Chapter 6. Preventing Tuberculosis

1. Eve Jacobs, "TB Roars Back," *HealthState*, University of Medicine and Dentistry of New Jersey (UMDNJ), Spring-Summer 1998, <http://www. mdnj.edu/umcweb/marketing_and_communications/publications/umdnj_magazine/hstate/sprsm98/tubercul.html> (February 21, 2005).

2. Barry E. Zimmerman and David J. Zimmerman, *Killer Germs* (Chicago: Contemporary Books, 1996), p. 72.

Chapter 7. Tuberculosis and the Future

1. Lee B. Reichman and Janice Hopkins Tanne, *Timebomb: The Global Epidemic of Multi-Drug-Resistant Tuberculosis* (New York: McGraw-Hill, 2001), p. 185.

2. Ibid.

3. Sarah Yang, "Gene mutation leads to super-virulent strain of TB, finds new study," *UC Berkeley News*, December 8, 2003, <http://www.berkeley.edu/news/media/releases/2003/12/08_mutation.shtml> (January 11, 2005).

4. Rachel Champeau and Natalie Waugh, "Clinical Trial of a New TB Vaccine in the U.S. Begins," *Aeras Global TB Vaccine Foundation*, February 17, 2004, <http://www.aeras.org/news/ releases/02172004.html> (January 11, 2005); Anne A. Oplinger, "First U.S. Tuberculosis Vaccine Trial in 60 Years Begins," *NIAID News*, January 26, 2004, <http://www2.niaid.nih.gov/newsroom/ releases/corixatbvac.htm> (January 11, 2005).

5. Lou Hirsh, "E-Nose Knows: Technology 'Smells' Bacteria," *Sci-Tech Today*, November 1, 2001, <http://sci.newsfactor.com/perl/story/14506.html> (January 11, 2005).

6. Sequella Incorporated, "Transdermal Patch," © 1997–2001, <http://www.sequella.com/pipeline/transdermal.asp> (January 11, 2005).

7. Charlene Crabb, "A New TB Drug by 2010: or Sooner?" *Bull World Health Organization* [online], June 2002, vol. 80, no. 6 [cited 26 August 2004], pp. 518–519, <http://www.scielosp.org/scielo.php?script=sci_arttext&pid=S0042-96862002000600022&lng=en&nrm=iso> (January 11, 2005).

8. A. Maureen Rouhl, "Paying Attention to Unmet Needs," *Chemical & Engineering News*, Vol. 80, No. 38, September 23, 2002, pp. 67–76.

9. Crabb.

10. Jon Cohen, "New TB Drug Promises Shorter, Simpler Treatment," *Science*, Vol. 306, December 10, 2004, p. 1872.

Glossary

active TB—A contagious form of TB, in which symptoms are present.

AIDS (acquired immune deficiency syndrome)—A viral disease in which the body's disease-fighting cells are damaged or destroyed. It is caused by infection by HIV.

alveoli (*sing.* alveolus)—The tiny air sacs in the lungs, in which gas exchange takes place.

BCG vaccine—A weakened form of *Mycobacterium bovis* used in most of the world to provide protection against tuberculosis.

bronchi (*sing.* bronchus)—The two large air tubes leading from the trachea into the lungs.

bronchioles—Smaller air tubes of the lungs that branch off from the bronchi.

cilia—Tiny hairlike structures on the cells in the membrane lining the respiratory passages; cilia beat back and forth to create an upward current in the mucus.

DNA (deoxyribonucleic acid)—A chemical that carries hereditary instructions that guide the formation and working of the cells and of the whole body.

dormant—Inactive, in a resting state.

DOTS (directly observed treatment, short-course)—A government-supported public health program requiring patients to take medications under observation by a health worker.

drug resistance—The ability of a disease germ to survive and multiply in the presence of a drug that would ordinarily kill or disable it; resistance to two or more drugs is known as multiple-drug resistance, or MDR.

false negative—A test result showing the absence of infection when it is actually present.

false positive—A test result indicating the presence of infection when there is none.

gene splicing—Isolating a piece of DNA and joining it to a DNA molecule of another organism.

HIV (human immunodeficiency virus)—The virus that causes AIDS.

immune system—The body's disease-fighting system, which includes the white blood cells.

immunity—Protection against a disease, even in the presence of the germs causing it.

infection—The presence of disease-producing germs in the body.

infectious disease—An illness that can be spread from one organism to another (such as from human to human or from animal to human) or from the environment to a human or animal.

larynx—Voice box.

latent TB—An inactive form of TB, in which the condition is not contagious and no symptoms are present.

lesion—A spot of tissue damage or abnormality caused by injury or disease; a wound or sore.

lobes—Parts or sections.

lung resection—A surgical procedure that involves removing a damaged part of the lung.

macrophages—Disease-fighting white blood cells that can eat and digest microorganisms.

Mantoux test—A test for TB in which purified tuberculin extract is injected under the skin; swelling after two to three days indicates a positive test.

meningitis—Inflammation of the meninges, the membranes covering the brain or spinal cord.

miliary tuberculosis—A rare form of TB in which small nodules are formed throughout the body.

mutation—A change in form or nature, especially a change in the genetic material (DNA).

mycobacteria—A group of bacteria including *Mycobacterium tuberculosis* (the tubercle bacillus), which causes pulmonary TB in humans, and *M. bovis*, which infects cows and humans and causes TB in bones and joints.

nodules—Lumps.

PCR (polymerase chain reaction) method—A diagnostic technique in which a piece of the germ's DNA is copied millions of times, which makes it possible to detect a single infected cell among thousands of uninfected cells.

pharynx—Throat.

pneumothorax—The presence of air or gas in the cavity around the heart and lungs as a result of injury or disease; a collapsed lung.

pulmonary—Having to do with the lungs.

pulmonary tuberculosis—Common form of TB in which tubercles form mainly in the lungs.

reactivation TB—Return of the initial TB infection.

recombinant vaccine—Vaccine that contains a piece of DNA from different species.

sanatorium—A health facility for rest, treatment, and rehabilitation of people with chronic diseases.

sputum—Mucus or pus that is expelled from the lungs (through spitting or coughing).

T cells—White blood cells that attack and kill invading germs or stimulate other cells to make antibodies.

trachea—Windpipe; breathing tube that connects the nose to the bronchi.

transdermal—Acting through the skin.

tubercle—A small, hard swelling in which invading TB bacteria are walled up.

tubercle bacilli—Tuberculosis-causing bacteria.

tuberculin—A liquid made from tubercle bacilli.

Further Reading

Books

Farrell, Jeanette. *Invisible Enemies: Stories of Infectious Diseases*. New York: Farrar, Straus, and Giroux, 2005.

Friedlander, Mark P., Jr. *Outbreak: Disease Detectives at Work*. Minneapolis: Lerner Publications Co., 2003.

Routh, Kristina. *Just the Facts: Tuberculosis*. Chicago: Heinemann Library, 2004.

Walker, Pam, and Elaine Wood. *The Respiratory System*. San Diego, Calif.: Lucent Books, 2003.

Yancey, Diane. *Tuberculosis*. Brookfield, Conn.: Twenty-First Century Books, 2001.

Internet Addresses

(See also **For More Information**, p. 94.)

NobelPrize.org. *Robert Koch and Tuberculosis.*
<http://nobelprize.org/educational_games/
medicine/tuberculosis/readmore.html>

World Health Organization. *Stop TB Partnership.*
<http://www.stoptb.org/>

World Health Organization. *Global Atlas of Infectious
Diseases: An Interactive Information and Mapping
System.*
<http://globalatlas.who.int>

Index